SATISFYING A WOMAN IN BED

Principle To Knowing Exactly What to do

BY

DAVID JOSEPH

TABLE OF CONTENT

Introduction

The majority of good sex involves teamwork. Men frequently rush the act and undervalue foreplay because they are unaware of how much women value it. Your wife may not be ready for the act simply because you are all heated up. You'll be off to a good start if you take a laid-back attitude and pay attention to what she wants. Women require these for a fulfilling and healthy sexual life. And don't make an effort to make her orgasm; frequently, the pleasure of the foreplay will do so, and she may or may not have another orgasm during intercourse.

In fact, studies show that men have penile-vaginal penetration orgasms more frequently than women, and just 34% to 40% of the time, women can experience an orgasm during sexual activity on their own. There, a myth debunked!

Chapter 1

It takes more than just getting an orgasm to satisfy a lady in bed. It combines flexibility, emotion, and foreplay. Giving your woman what she wants won't be an issue for you if you know exactly what you're doing. However, there is a potential that your partner might be lying if you are unsure of your skills. It only requires a deeper comprehension of your companion and her requirements.

Your sexual life will continue to be exciting and vibrant for a very long time as long as you prioritize your partner's sexual demands over your own, and remember to keep sex fresh.

Why it's important to satisfy a woman in bed

Sadly, a lot of men are known for the "wham, bam, thank you ma'am" sexual routine. In other words, they are selfish. All they really care about is their pleasure and getting their own orgasm.

But do you really think that would satisfy a woman in bed? Do you really think that she's that much of a "giver" that she doesn't care about feeling good herself?

Of course not!

One of the reasons men tend to be selfish in bed is because it takes longer to turn a woman on than it does for him to get turned on himself. He thinks that her body reacts as quickly as his, so he doesn't think she needs extra stimulation. But she

And that's where most guys get lazy. It takes effort and a lot of "work" to satisfy a woman in bed and make her orgasm. But that doesn't mean it's difficult.

Some women are easier to please than others, but all of them deserve a man who makes them sexually satisfied.

How long does it take to satisfy a woman in bed?

The answer you are probably hoping to hear is – immediately! But that's not the case. As I just said, women are slower to get turned on and to orgasm. Plus, what one woman likes, another might not.

Some women know their bodies well, and so they do just what it takes to orgasm. While others don't know at all. What that means is that satisfying one woman could happen right away. And with others, she may never be fully satisfied. So, there's no clear-cut answer to this question. You're just going to have to put in the effort and gauge her reaction to see how satisfied she seems to be at any given moment.

Sexual And Emotional Gratification

You should be aware that for women, emotional intimacy plays a significant role in determining sexual happiness.

Two individuals can get together and have fantastic sex for a while, after all.

However, boredom will quickly set in and the thrill of passionate sex will start to go away quickly.

Chapter 2

The strongest sexual organ that humans have is not found in our underwear, despite what you may have previously heard.

In our minds, the brain is the part of your body that contributes the most to amazing sex, more so than any other part.

The likelihood is high that every other area of your body will concur with your thinking if you are experiencing amazing sex. You must first learn to make your partner's mind love what you do in bed in order to have absolutely fantastic sex and make her feel satisfied. Her emotions will follow after her intellect is enjoying it, and then her body will do the same.

You don't need to stay in the act longer or work harder to please your woman; all you need to do is concentrate on making it enjoyable for both of you

Start off with a kiss

Beginning with a kiss is the finest technique to satisfy a woman in bed. Most women enjoy receiving kisses on their lips, boobs, necks, and other parts of their bodies. For her, more is better.

A kiss can be a lethal weapon (one with health benefits too). Use it ferociously and passionately to arouse her senses.

Every woman has a few unique erogenous zones that can be kissed to rapidly turn her on. Find those regions on her body by nibbling, then keep them in mind for the next time. A woman might be sexually gratified by having kisses placed all over her body. Make sure this tip is at the top of your list if you're seeking for foreplay advice to improve your sex.

If you want to please your woman, prolonged foreplay does wonders.

Patience and build-up are crucial when pleasing a woman. Beautiful bodies are a blessing for women. There is a lot of ground to cover, you should also strive to achieve that. To arouse her, you essentially need to become an expert at foreplay. This will work like magic if you wait before you penetrate her. While you're at it, why not add a little role play to take things up a notch? You could order sexy lingerie for her or get yourselves both fun and exciting costumes that can heighten up the excitement and make your act really last.

Don't be a slob in bed.

Recognize the distinction between passion and abuse. Do not go over the edge and offend her. A rough love session shouldn't be violent; it should be crazy. Asking for her permission and establishing healthy sexual boundaries are the greatest ways to make sure she feels comfortable. Stop making out with your partner right away if they start to feel uneasy at any stage. No means no. The simplest answer to how to make sex better for her is to ask her what she likes or if she is enjoying what you're doing, read her body language cues, and follow her lead rather than just presuming that you know your way around her body and are showing her the time of her life.

To spice up your sexual life, use dirty words

Learn the art of dirty talking if you want to satisfy a woman in bed. Don't overdo it with your description, though. Instead, discuss with her your favorite aspects of her, how seeing her naked makes you feel, your fantasies for her, and other things. You can also use dirty dancing to entice your partner and restart your regular sex. This gives sex a new attraction and makes it feel like the first time. The goal is to make her feel content in bed. Being sexually desired is pretty gratifying, and the secret to satisfying a woman is to make her feel needed and desired.

Whisper romantic things

Whispering something pleasant and seductive into a woman's ear repeatedly while she is in bed is one of the best bedtime tactics. Say something seductive as you nibble on her ear. Surprise her with some sensual lines as you kiss her lips. Talk to her about your fantasies and get her excited. She will be greatly aroused by this. The art of seduction involves much more than just applying pressure to the proper areas to induce a female orgasm. The real seduction frequently starts outside of the bedroom and starts with the head. It might be time to start thinking outside the box if you want to really blow her mind with your techniques.

Having oral sex

After some sustained foreplay, try surprising her by introducing oral sex to the mix. Even penetrative sex is not as enjoyable for her as this. It is seen to be the best way to delight a lady and there are various ways to orally excite her during sex. Take a cue from Fifty Shades of Grey and grab her, play with her, lick her, bite her—there are so many things you can do!

Giving her head when she least expects it can cause her to experience levels of pleasure you haven't seen her achieve before, much as how a spontaneous BJ can really bring the heat up for you.

Again, the most important thing is to take your time and avoid rushing. If you do it perfectly, you won't have to worry about how to make your girl feel satisfied in bed.

Please your woman by teasing and licking her

Play with her body and run your hands over it. Caress her and tickle her in a few spots. Massage her breasts or stimulate her down there. Don't forget to make good use of your tongue to tease her. A little bit of licking will do wonders and your woman will respond beautifully to these moves. Softly bite the folds of her skin and watch her moan with pleasure. Hitting these pressure points for female orgasm will instantly take the heat up several notches.

Besides, there are several fun products and toys that can heighten the fun of exploring her body with your tongue. For instance, there is something called flavored kissing dust that you can sprinkle all over her body and lick it off, making every pore in her body come alive with excitement.

Go for a quickie

It's not necessary to always operate at full throttle. When you want to sexually, please a girl, the element of surprise is excellent. Catching her off guard (and in strange settings) might result in a truly heated session. She can be doing a chore when you give her a passionate kiss. In an instant, things would get out of hand, and she would be panting and begging for more.

One of the things women need for a happy and healthy sex life is a feeling of being desired and seeing their partner hunger for them and never get enough of them. Nothing conveys all of this better than a quickie that says "I've got to have you here and now." Of course, even though the intent here is to express your passion and desire, make sure you don't disregard her consent in the process.

Dress well and smell good to please your woman

Hygiene matters when setting the tone for good sex. Before heading to bed, take a shower and wear a soft perfume. Make sure that bodily and pubic hair is all removed or trimmed. Pay attention to your undergarments. Most importantly, brush your teeth well. This will set the mood quite nicely; no one can enjoy sex if their partner smells bad. Avoid making such mistakes in bed.

It is often seen that spouses become so used to each other that they stop putting in efforts completely. When husbands wonder why the spark is gone, the most probable answer is this. You can't please your wife during sex without putting in the basic efforts of hygiene.

Ask her what she likes

Asking your woman how she would like to be loved is preferable to pushing your will on her. Put her wants and needs before your own. Give weight to the things and methods she values. In a relationship, being sexually generous is absolutely necessary. This will assist your woman in letting go of her inhibitions and respond to your fundamental inquiries about how to completely fulfill a woman in bed.

Allowing a woman to take the lead could be one of the secrets to gratifying her. Tell her that you will merely follow her lead because she is in charge.

Ask her to express through her words and/or actions where she wants you to go or what she wants you to do. You'll be able to tell what she finds most enjoyable as she assumes a dominant role in sex, and it will also help her let go of her inhibitions and embrace her sexual impulses.

Try making out at different places

Don't restrict yourself to the bedroom; explore other locations in the house like the kitchen, study or even bathroom. You may even try outdoor sex to experience that rush of adrenaline. It will be a refreshing change of pace and locale; a little sexual adventure keeps things feisty in the relationship.

If things have become a little predictable and monotonous in the bedroom and you're wondering how to make sex better for her, perhaps consider taking a short sexcation. Find a nice hotel or resort nearby, book a room, and get away from the weekend with nothing more than a change of clothes, some lingerie, sex toys, and experience your sex life come alive with passion.

Try using sensual food to satisfy a woman in bed

Keep a stock of chocolate sauce to turn on the heat. Instead of licking the sauce from a plate, try pouring it over her twins and slowly lick it. Literally, nothing could be sexier than this. There are many dirty games you can play with food. Use fruit, whipped cream, honey, and even caramel for an unforgettable night of pleasure.

Love and romance win the day

Remember this tip to satisfy women in bed. A woman loves to be loved before you undress her for a full-on lovemaking session. Romance her and make her feel special before you start exploring her body. This will ensure that she is completely engrossed with you in bed. Work her hottest erogenous zones to make her orgasm. And after you're done having sex, stay in bed and cuddle her.

Get a little naughtier to please your wife during sex

Ask her what her wildest fantasies are and try to fulfill them. If she wants to try out something new like a threesome, then give it a shot. This might make things sexier for the two of you as you turn those wild dreams into reality. This is a great way of tackling boredom in the relationship or marriage. Of course, you must try this only if you are completely comfortable. Remember at times jealousy can creep up and make things messier.

Bonus Tip

The most important tip is to let her orgasm before you do. If you have an orgasm before she does, chances are she will have to make do without one. Work on controlling your erection better, hold on in there and let her have the first high point in your lovemaking session. Even if she doesn't orgasm during intercourse, don't let that leave you feeling dejected or disappointed.

Key Pointers

- For women, emotional connection and closeness are key components of sexual pleasure.

- The true pleasure centers for a woman lie outside of her vagina, therefore foreplay is essential for fulfilling her.

- The secret to your partner's sexual fulfillment is to listen to what she wants and take your time to offer her an enjoyable experience.

- You must express your passion and desire, but do not go against her wishes.

- To improve sex for women, keep in mind that seduction starts in the head and outside of the bedroom.